STATIONS
The Way of the Cross

STATIONS
The Way of the Cross

Text by
DANIEL BERRIGAN

Terra Cotta Reliefs by
MARGARET PARKER

1817

Harper & Row, Publishers, San Francisco

New York, Cambridge, Philadelphia, St. Louis
London, Singapore, Sydney, Tokyo

FIRST EDITION

Library of Congress Cataloging-in-Publication Data

Berrigan, Daniel.
    Stations: the way of the cross.

    1. Jesus Christ—Passion—Meditations.   2. Stations of the
Cross—Meditations.   I. Parker, Margaret,
1947–   .   II. Title.

BT431.B43   1989   232.9′6   88-45680
ISBN 0-06-060766-1

---

89 90 91 92 93 HC 10 9 8 7 6 5 4 3 2 1

CONTENTS

PREFACE

The tradition that inspired Margaret Parker's Stations has a long history in popular piety. And like most such devotions, this one raises certain perplexing questions.

The Holy Land, the holy places. Indeed, the words have a most unholy history, drenched as they are in blood—and not only the blood of Christ: the bloodletting of one entrenched side by the other has usually been caused by fervent believers waging war (invariably declared *just* or *holy* by either side).

Moreover, the history of war, including religious war, is by no means canceled. To say the least. Neither Christians nor Moors, as far as can be judged from El Salvador or Palestine, have embraced nonviolence in the image of their God. The bloodshed continues to this dreadful hour, as we know.

Palestine-Israel: what a history of blood prodigally shed! In the first instance, the blood of Christ; in the last—yesterday, today, tomorrow—the blood of children, of the aged, of anyone.

Blood, we are told, is holy in Jewish and Christian tradition. Whether applied to the Savior or to a Palestinian child, all blood is holy; it is the very rubric of life, the sign and seal of the God of life.

But back to the ambiguous history of the Stations of the Cross.

We learn that the devotion arose as the aftermath of a feverish wave agitating late medieval Europe. Palestine, the Holy Land, had been taken by the Moors. Crisis indeed: the soil Christ walked seized by infidel hands!

It could not be borne. Bernard of Clairvaux, a monk with a warrior soul and a tongue of stinging fire, became a symbol of the Christian movement. He preached in favor of what came to be known, for immediate good and eventual ill, as a Crusade. One thinks of an old-fashioned religious revival, dangerously puffed into a holy war.

God wills it! went the cry. Reclaim the holy places! The troops assembled: the blessing was invoked on behalf of those who would die (and kill) in blessed combat.

Arab fundamentalism? No, Christian.

But then a question arose. What of those who for one reason or another were prevented from direct participation in the holy undertaking? Should they not also win a blessing, by proxy? There were the aged, the ill, the children (though later, caught up in the tidal wave, the children too marched from Europe eastward, and died).

In any case, an inspired decision was reached by church authorities; noncombatant Christians could be Crusaders-at-home. They too could be included in the blessing.

Thus our Stations of the Cross.

Hence too the ambiguity, the nagging questions.

Was not a sanguinary Christianity being blessed? A sense that war must be made total? That everyone, by one means or another, must be drawn into an atmosphere both violent and virtuous? That those unable to kill (but in principle *willing* to kill) should harbor, even nurture, killing thoughts, should have a large part in bloody affairs, and a reward as well?

Please note the irony. Above all other places named holy, Jerusalem was to be returned to Christian control— by military might.

It was in Jerusalem that the Savior counseled Peter to "put up your sword," adding ominously, "Those who live by the sword, perish by the sword."

Such counsel implied a price to be paid. In the case of Jesus, that price was a savage death at the hands of the powers.

Jerusalem, the city literally marked by the bloodletting of God, was to be reclaimed, by whatever means, by the "faithful."

In two ways, really. On the one hand, the warriors were to be rewarded for what came to be known as the "supreme sacrifice" (of their own lives, of the lives of others). In effect, they were promised heaven in place of the hell they had helped create.

Those who remained at home for valid reasons could also march, to a different drummer. They could, as it were, undergo the rigors (and rewards) of the Crusade— though in a less rigorous way. They could merit a like blessing by "making the Stations."

Shortly, images were set up in churches and cathedrals—images of the Savior's pilgrimage of shame, from Pilate's court through his death and burial. Processions formed: the faithful trod from image to image. At each, prayers were spoken, hymns sung, periods of silence observed. Out of the devotion arose an art stressing the pathetic and literal sufferings of the Savior and his mother. One thinks of the sublime threnody of the Virgin, the "Stabat Mater," composed in the same period.

Thus the Passion of Christ, the central Christian story, was both dramatized and domesticated.

Thus too, in a stroke of genius, political, military, and economic interests were melded in the furnace of religious fervor. God wills it! Could there be a nobler credential for the sacking of a city, the taking of captives, the wounding and killing?

Thus two worlds, separated by seas and continents, were joined in a single current of ecstatic faith. In a highly charged symbolic sense, as well as in a bloody military sense, the "holy places" were laid claim and liberated by believers. The bread of children, so to speak, was snatched from infidel dogs and placed in rightful hands.

And thus the ironies. They strike like lightning.

In the Crusaders' duffels, in the holds of the ships, behold the cargo, spiritual and carnal, the body and heart of that war called holy. Indispensable items: slogans; invocations of God; images cast in metal; cloth scapulars; avaricious purses (bulking larger on return than on embarking); diaries vivid with liberation fervor, triumphalism, and papal approval; crosses fore and aft; the sword; the incantation "God wills it." And then certain key words, juxtaposed like lowered visors glowering eye to eye: "Christian warriors," "Moslem dogs."

These items were domestic necessities also. They were in large supply at home as well as abroad.

In such wise, and so outfitted, the Church, whether in distant places, on boisterous seas, or at home in Europe, followed, as was fondly thought, in the very footsteps of the Savior.

So the Christians thought.

In judging the spirit of the devotions and the battles, in assessing the behavior the devotions inspired and the battles executed, one must leave much to the mercy of God.

Half bewildered must our Christ be, as the honors accorded him are steeped in the dishonor of violence. Blood—today as then in that perpetually fevered Holy Land—will have blood.

But in this book we come on something else—on a more peaceable and befitting theme: the Passion of Christ and the homeless of our world.

In New York the theme is too close for comfort. The icons of Margaret Parker, terrible in their gentleness, come to life in streets and doorways and subways, in the impermanent shelters that are halfway houses on the trek of misery. The tormented, lost wanderers of our city are all about us; they huddle, sleep, awaken, stagger about, hold out their beggar hands. We wear their presence like a great societal shroud—our own. In them that other city, a city of shame, stirs to life. Day and night.

In this sense, which art makes bearable, no one of us is apart from the action. We follow the "Stations of the homeless" with every step we take in public, in every neighborhood, on our way to jobs and shops and theaters and parks. No neighborhood exempted, none off limits—the poorest, the most posh.

Thus the homeless dramatize, as the images of Margaret Parker remind us, something of great import to spiritual understanding. The homeless live out, in dreadful, literal detail, the poverty we would rather conceal—from God, from ourselves. They are icons of the "other side" of ourselves; they are icons of modern life turned inside out. That shroud again, its seams and rents shamefully exposed.

Their language—their curses and ravings, their un-
accountable silence—is a code. It is a totting up of the
cost: the lives we lead, the lives we long to lead. Lives
of appetite, envy, racism—that "good life" so com-
mended to all, so lethal and leveling; the cost of weap-
ons and waste and war, the fuel of the great voracious
urban engine.

The homeless are the shadow at the heart of things,
the shadow we flee. It is named death.

Filth, garbage bags, smells, dragging carts, lost
looks—these are props of the drama of the all-but-lost:
ourselves. Their props are the decor of an anticreation,
created by ourselves. Created by conspicuous consump-
tion, by condos and cruises, by Standard Oil, by Navy-
port, by a frozen war budget, by great communicators
and audacious liars, by wheelers and dealers and silk-
suited lawless thieves.

But this is not the whole story. If it were, if the homeless were no more than the drones of a dying hive, a
lost tribe of unrelieved and permanent misery, if they
did no more than tell us how deeply we are stuck, no art
could come of this. And Margaret Parker would be well
advised to take up the themes of celebrational despair,
so dear to the trendy pimps of downtown Manhattan
galleries.

There is more, so much more. Her art has tenderly
and truthfully conveyed that more.

She offers us images of faith—the faith that keeps on
keeping on. She endows her street people with dignity
beyond words. In defeat and moral darkness (our own),
she strikes a light and holds it to these faces. She sets
one apart on a bench, a veritable *mater dolorosa* of

Fourth Street. She grants another the merciful shoulder of a Simon of Cyrene, heaving the cart uphill. Yet another knows the momentary healing touch of a hand on the face. (And in a stroke of stunning insight, the needy one also raises a hand to heal the healer.) And finally, two children, terribly matured in the maelstrom of the streets, in tenderness cover the dead.

These gestures are pure gift. They are the gift of the poor—to one another, to ourselves.

From another point of view, such images do not belong: they shock, they lie outside the patrimony of the culture. The kindnesses of kinship, I call such gestures. Through them, Parker refuses the self-injected quick fix, the despair of those who, tooth and claw, prowl the affluent jungle, claiming and killing.

All is not lost, she insists. Even such as we might be salvaged.

Strangely enough, through her images the streets become also a school of mercy. There we might learn unaccustomed skills. There, against all likelihood, we might learn compassion. Might set beating once more the dormant heartbeat of a permanent winter.

Daniel Berrigan

STATIONS
The Way of the Cross

STATION ONE

Condemned

O Lord, how my adversaries have increased!
Many are rising up against me.
Many are saying of my soul,
"There is no deliverance for him in God."
But you, O Lord, are a shield about me.
My glory, the One who lifts my head.

(Psalm 3:1–3)

The thump of a gavel
("vagrancy   loitering")
JOHN DOE, DEFENDANT
his look   a man condemned
drummed out of the world
That look
ice   fire   bewilderment   despair—
look at him   looking at us!

His crime
No possessions   no property
no equity   no income   no credit
no account
The ultimate affront
(the immaculate myth
the "twin fetishes"   stability   order)

3

The defendant   hunches forward
not toward the judge
(justice misserved   hopeless)
he knows his fate
thump of gavel   judge   guardian
of who owns what
(of what owns whom)

That look   pierces to the quick

The hammer comes down
Take him away!   away!

Justice must be served
(property must be served
taxes   Caesar)
Take him away!

Nameless   on his way   *via dolorosa*
Where the friends   the disciples?
No one   not one
empty   benches
like graves awaiting   twelve dead men
The judge   lord Pilate
Caesar's right arm   hammer of god
And high above
a stone   throne   cenotaph
on which is graved
The Law!   The Law!

Nevertheless
say it
Today's charge   today's crime
neither vagrancy   loitering   whatever
The crime   speaking clumsily
"propertylessness"

As to our defendant
Behold the man!

How dare he
assault and batter
the above-mentioned
scheme   scam   neat arrangement   dream
Verily   Speedily   Away with him!

STATION TWO

The Cross

Surely our griefs he himself bore,
And our sorrows he carried;
Yet we ourselves esteemed him stricken,
Smitten of God, and afflicted.

(Isaiah 53:4)

So we begin   corner
Second Avenue and Nameless Street
John Doe   takes up his cross
gleans   from city trash
stale half-rotted provender
Sufficient unto the day
the garbage thereof

The scene   (puzzling   adversarial)
back-to-back
the well-heeled   the set faces
movers and shakers
in a minor key
They move   they move things   they move on
(By no means evildoers   in the grand mode
even the minor mode)
Simply
other matters weigh (on them   on us)

Concentrated   (distracted)
single-minded   muddle-headed
In the rockbound city   carving a place
Investment   property   "marketable skills"
Everything
(the world   the times   the street   all
too much with them   with us)

They wear for phiz
that granite New York mask—
behind which   the vulnerable heart
tossed night and day   on a spit of fury
may   for time
with luck and pluck   make it
breathe free

They lend not a glance   stride past
into a void?
in any case
past   that figure
skinny as a shadow
(the inarticulate
frozen fury   the city
maker and breaker)
faceless   nameless creature
bending above   mere trash
his mere life   trashed—
he sifts the offal
flotsam   urban debris
hither and yon blown
yesterday's stale news
"In City   Homeless Multiply"   etc.

Eccolo!
folded in   like leaven in dough—
eccolo!   the "new creation"
two specimens   side-by-side
(misery   the good life)
Thus   the human
ourselves   "image of God"
altered   narrowed
(two only exemplars)
reductive misery
and moral shrug

Choose?
refuse!
Cry out   create
other epiphanies   pauses
dances   rainbows   delights!

———————

It is told how the blessed Saint Martin of Tours,
encountering one winter's day a beggar shivering in the
cold, and the saint on horseback and warmly clad,
Martin did straightway dismount. Then seizing his
sword, he cut his fine cloak in two, wrapped the
miserable man in the better half and himself in the
other. He embraced the man, mounted his horse, and
proceeded on his way.

That night in a dream, our Lord Christ appeared to
him, clothed in half a cloak, saying, "Martin, you this
day succored your Savior in pitiful guise. For which
favor, know you have found grace with God."

———————

Maybe the word to
achievers   is
"Come down   come down
dismount your high horse!"
Lend a glance   lend a hand
For surely   large questions
touchy matters   loom
even at that height

Lost to us then   that
imaginative glance?   that
mindfulness   that
heart unforeclosed?   that
small word   "Something can be done"   that
small resolve   "I should do something"   that
insistence   groaning toward birth—
this "filthy rotten system"
excess battening   misery multiplied
greed and need   appetite   deprivation—
this must go?

Must go!
also
the tags   reductive   contemptuous
dishonoring the human—
"all but garbage"   "guilty passerby"
a better calling   beckons
better semblance   resemblance
of the human

Turn   turn   turn
toward   toward   toward
never away
never away from
never away   from You

STATION THREE

He Falls

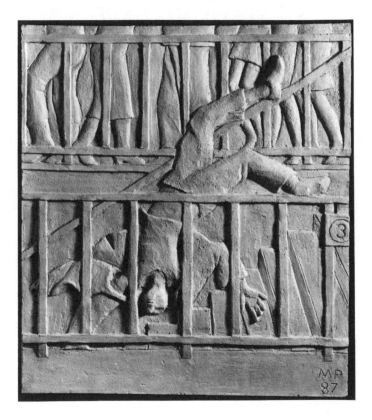

Those who see me in the street flee from me.
I am forgotten as a dead man, out of mind,
I am like a broken vessel.

(Psalm 31:11–12)

"NUMBER 3 TRAIN   BROADWAY EXPRESS   ENTERING
  THE STATION!"
Rush hour   cave of instant chaos
Someone   shadowy   dun
ever so slowly
hesitant as a sleepwalker
mounts   the stairs
feeling his way   then
awful!
nondescript   sack of misery
falling   tumbling
head over heels   over and down

They glance
they pass by
Well   he lost it years ago
fell   fell out of good graces   out of the city
out of the world
let the cops handle it   bundle him off

A thunder of footfalls   says it
Who we are
who we are not
legs   locomotion   inanition
click and shuffle and get there fast
irresponsible
shrug-in-passing

Answered in the asking
the question   forbidden
under pain   of original murder—
"Am I my brother's keeper?"

Time's captives   bound to the wheel
that grinds us under
frozen   in motion
powerless   to pause   savor   listen
never
"the world   in a grain of sand
eternity   in an hour"
neither flower nor sunlight
breaking through   gently
the heart's rank soil
No
but time's grind and grimace—
one or another
nameless   fallen
off the wheel of Ixion—
what matter
who cares

!NUMBER 3 EXPRESS!   !WATCH CLOSING DOORS!
Inadvertent
hurried and harried
Alas for the loss—
right reason   compassion
gone gone   lurching tail light
wind   soiled newsprint
rising witless   hell's stale bad news
yesterday   haunting today
today   mocking tomorrow

Where
where are our faces gone?
look for them   all but in vain
One face only
fallen fallen
low
grit and filth
For the rest
a headless herd   and its thunder

Let us pray
Forgive our trespasses
trespassing over   around   beside
the fallen brother
Forgive   forgive
scrambled minds   slavish lives
witless errands
Forgive us who fall
away from tenderness
tumble down
down from our calling

"The son came to his senses. He said, ' . . . I will rise and go to my father.' When he was yet far off, the father saw him, was moved to compassion. He ran and embraced him and kissed him. 'Let us eat and be merry,' he said, 'for this my son was dead and has come to life again; he was lost, and has been found.' And they began to make merry."

(Luke 15:17–18, 20, 23–24)

Grant us   a return
beckon   compel us
For tender sake   of a fallen brother
grant us   a saving pause
succoring hands   lost tenderness
We would not forever
stream by
pell mell in pursuit   of all
we want   and want not

STATION FOUR

The Mother

Is it nothing to you all who pass this way?
Look, see if there is any sorrow like my sorrow.

(Lamentations 1:12)

Number 4 train   reels   thunders by
crowded   to the doors
Summon
loneliness   tenderness
dignity   self-possession
Mother of Him   who thrice fell
unde origo   inde salus
(our salvation   born of her)

Today   this sorrowful day
homeless mother
Via dolorosa
Welter of faces   ricochet of lives
chancy embraces
fear-ridden distancings

Resolute
she turns her back
sits enthroned
queen of near nothing—
nondescript clothing
a coverlet against
the season's distemper
Thus   in one life

the teeming world
its voracious maw
is tamed   reproved

How   how has she   come to this
pure inwardness
aching   unvoiced   a cry—
rides the air
Would that   beside her stood
son   companion   lover
All   all are gone
swept into darkness
The brute train vanishes
she sits   regent of misery
Lost lost   to her
the heart's grip and tug
the heart's life line

Hands   feet
like Zen icons—
the hand turns toward
invitational   beckoning
hand   of a working woman
hard   thankless   long   the labors
creating
order   amid disorder
cleanliness   amid squalor

No sniveling beggar
she wears defeat   like a royal mantle
That hand
direct as a glance   viewing the viewer
a commanding gesture

She the mother   of moral reversal
stern invention
exceeds the eyes' blink
the rash conclusion—
("victim   nobody")
Take her in account!
among the great ones
primal ones   ancestors
a spirit beyond reckoning
surpassing wondrously
the squalid world

About her   raging
pandemonium
(the not yet arrived   the never quite here)
She   alone
takes to herself   wraps around
like a scarf of being—
rest   arrival
the "still point"
claims for herself
the moment's substance
drinks deep
from streams of being

"The spirit of wisdom is intelligent, holy, unique, subtle, agile, penetrating, pure, lucid, the friend of all goodness, not to be coerced, kin of the human, constant in purpose, without guile."

(Wisdom 7:22)

Mother Courage! Mother of sorrows!
sufficient   unto herself
stasis of nondesire—
having lost all
what remains to lose?

We   whom desire
daily makes sport of
launching us hither
deporting us yon
forever outsiders
to self-possession
to sweetness and strength—
Pray for us Mother—
still our vagaries
distill our desires

"Great God, grant me to know this one who shares your throne. For I am weak in vision and my life escapes me. Justice is beyond me, and comprehension. . . . If I fall short of this wisdom of hers, I am reduced to nothing. Let her dwell at my side, and mourn with me."

(Wisdom 9:4–6,10)

STATION FIVE

The Helper

By chance a certain priest was going down that road. And when he saw the man who had fallen among thieves, he passed by on the other side.

Likewise a Levite, when he came to the place and saw him, passed by on the other side.

But a certain Samaritan who was on a journey came upon him; and when he saw him, he was moved with compassion. He came to him, bandaged up his wounds, put him on his own beast, and brought him to an inn, and took care of him.

(Luke 10:31–34)

No excuses   no "pressing business"
a certain parity   perhaps
Samaritan   or black   ("bin down so long
it looks   like up to me")   simpatico certainly
and above all   common sense
falling down is not   staying down
No   pick up the pieces
get moving again

Against the wall
a sign posted   half in
half outside the image—
"5 c SA—"   could it read
"five cent sale"?
And if so   a question arises
What conceivable object
of beauty   utility

is bought or sold today
for five inflated cents?

The sign   a subtle hint
a hideous price tag
stamped   on a life?
A vagrant   throwaway man
so nearly worth   nothing
(say   five inflated cents)
as to make no difference?

Yet   someone named Simon
declared
dramatized
the price he granted
someone   a near no one
an officially   worthless one
devalued   scorned
within hours   condemned
to pay   pay up
a price beyond reckoning
for "crimes against the state"

Caesar's   "5 cent SA—"
on the streets
on death rows
in ghettos
in abortion mills
"lives of no value"   up for sale
cheap   wholesale
all sales final!

Now and again
someone   the victim
turns   turns
the stigma around—
"This is my body,   given for you
my blood   shed for you"
Something
beyond price   wild freedom
cannot be seized
degraded   devalued

And then this Simon
pushing the cart along
turning things around
sized things up
out of the blue   came forward
no virtuous heavy breathing
spontaneous   combustion of heart
"Man's in trouble
hey there bro   let me give a hand"

Ragged arm below
brawny arm above—
hardly a word spoken
communion   the common task
Then   brute necessity—
("Move it along there!
no loitering!")
—yielding to freedom

––––––––––

"Which of these three, do you think, proved to be a neighbor to the man who fell into the robbers' hands? And he said, 'The one who showed mercy toward him.' And Jesus said to him, 'Go and do likewise.' "

(Luke 10:36)

––––––––––

STATION SIX

Compassion

He had no beauty or majesty to attract us to him,
nothing in his appearance that we should desire him.
   He was despised and rejected by all, a man of
sorrows, and familiar with suffering.
   Like one from whom we hide faces
he was despised, and we esteemed him not.

(Isaiah 53:2–3 NIV)

Mutuality
The woman lifts a glove
"size 6"
The harried   homeless one
mauled in the mad streets
so little to offer   nothing to offer
Nevertheless
he lifts a hand   toward her face
reticent
a grateful echo
a purgatorial   "thank you"

The glove   the veiled hand—
"a medically prudent procedure"?
"Could it be   do we have here
   the unspeakable AIDS?"
Let us presume   a "worst case"
bring the unmentionable   to light
purgation of terror

Christ figure?   with AIDS?
Christ   Worst case?
Beware   *procul este*
that realm   shame and death
signified by
Stations of the Cross

Like it or not   behold the Man!
(we like it   not at all)
stuck
with this intractable suffering One
his halts   and starts   and falls   and shame
demonic   daily   hourly
the urban   Stations of the Cross
via dolorosa

Objections rise
like sweat on the skin—
is it not the virtue of art
(the virtue of religion)
to "distance us"
from realities
too harsh for bearing?

O grant us a gesture
words   words   words   the failure deepens
O grant a gesture
original   spare   piercing to the quick
consequential

Once   on a Friday   we dare name "Good"
a woman   Veronica
(*vera ikon*   true image)
removed her veil
pressed it gently
against that torment
A gesture   spare   piercing
above all   consequential
The cloth   drawn away   *eccolo!*
true image   *vera ikon*   impressed there

Who hearkens   who cares?
her soul cries
I must   I must

Mutuality
mutual word   gesture
Prevenient   the unafflicted
(Hand outstretched   hand's glove)
Response
more difficult
for the unafflicted
proudly in place—
(come down   come down)—

Then   marvelous
the afflicted one
mimes   matches
(wordless   for wordless)
Action   reaction
incomprehensible
to pride   to ego
dispensing   largesse
unchallengeable
controllable   sweet   charity

Station 6
unsettling
the lightest of strokes—
a mysterious   *quid pro quo*
the afflicted one   *vera ikon*   cries out—
"I too am human!"

In giving   we are given
mystery   interplay
the wordless dance

If we attend
the hidden music
the wordless look
If we close eyes
breathe deep
leap
out and out
out of routine

out of ego
(out of sweet skin)—
our hand on a face
a hand on our face—
O ecstatic!
we shall see
and at last
be seen!

He Falls Again

O Lord, you have brought up my soul from hell;
You have kept me alive, that I should not go down
to the pit.

(Psalm 30:3)

Two arms   rise straight up
fall   in empty air
futile   helpless
down   down   once more   *via dolorosa*
maelstrom   chaos   scattered belongings
"things fall apart   the center cannot hold"

The burden   we groan under—
belongings   possessions
They fall away   See them go
Let them go   Let go

Letting go
unwelcome image   the rub—
Not only the poor   let go
a law   Zen law
law of   good sense
Let go   Let come   Let be

What holds firm?
debris   incoherence   incapacity   numbing
The grand scheme of things
unraveling before our eyes
the "grand alliances"   faith and reason
compassion and justice   peace within and worldly
breaking up   gone on the winds

Two arms only   a drowning man
face   form   lost   lost
out of time and place
out of the picture
utensils fall   pins and needles   minims
that "rag and bone shop of the heart"
tossed on high
a witless cyclone

Muttering in his beard   wild-eyed
pushing life ahead
a surf   against stone
Then
struck down
those tawdry   pitiful   "belongings"
shamefully exposed   their sum value
a "number 7" safety pin—
"lives of no value"

Do we conjure him   sight unseen
arms aloft
spasm   loss and despair
wildly reaching after
those tossing   floating trivia
weightless   tumbleweeds
surreal in the blue
junk shop aloft?

Is this the artful fiction
Or
does he lie prone   motionless   brought low
all   all
scattered pell mell about
horrid   inedible
savage street menu
death   the maître d'

Dead or alive?
Alive   it is decreed
(the story's   harsh discipline)
He must stand again—

To lose and lose   is not yet the end
Into further depth   summoned
further heights
You have lost everything?
You have not lost everything
"I will show you   the last thing"

"Why is light given to the one who suffers,
And life to the bitter of soul, Who long for death, but
   there is none,
And dig for it more than for hidden treasures; Who
   rejoice greatly,
They exult, when they find the grave? Why is light
given to one whose way is hidden,
And whom God has hedged in?"

(Job 3:20)

Sometimes   the barest word
cut to the bone
remains to us
losses recouped   or not
help at hand   or withheld
No matter
we must stand again
for the sake of children
for the sake of the forsaken
for no discernible reason
no sense   that makes sense
to ourselves   least of all

Pick up the pieces!
pieces of heart
pieces of memory
bits   pieces of love
once a whole cloth   proud tegument
ornament of life—
rags   bones   tatters
Pick up!
Go on!   More to come!

I do not know
whose lips utter the command
whose finger points   a way
a cloud of unknowing
a way   that is no way
a way
that makes   of the pilgrims—
who   despite all   go on   and on
going on   and on
perplexed   crestfallen
—makes of such   to worldly skulls
manifest losers   veriest fools
Of such matters   I know nothing
they are   "hidden from mine eyes"

———

"Blessed are you who have not seen, and have believed."

(John 20:29)

———

One thing holds firm
hold it firm
The promise holds

———————

"I am with you always."

(Matthew 28:20)

———————

STATION EIGHT

The Women

But Jesus turning to them said, "Daughters of Jerusalem, stop weeping for me, but weep for yourselves and for your children."

(Luke 23:28 NIV)

The Number 8 bus
Jerusalem-bound   grinds to a halt
A sorry passenger—
bedroll   umbrella   ragged clothing
down the aisle   staggers
under the jolting   thrum of motor
homeless   odoriferous   strap-hanger
He shatters the calm   discommodes
the daughters of Jerusalem

Every daughter like   every other daughter!
coifs alike   identical garb
souls alike!   soul mates!

Tears?   identical tears?
if they fall   at all—
fruitless!
His right hand
stretches toward them
entreaty   compassion—
the hand that healed   blind   halt   deaf
that raised the dead—
can His hand avail   heal?

The haunting   liberating
shadow of that hand!

Who will grant
daughters of Jerusalem
(their sons   daughters)
a soul of flesh
(graven   alas   where we sit
stand   walk   weep
tears   unavailing)

Likeness   unlikeness
(likelihood   unlikelihood)
The daughters of Jerusalem
hear   gentle reproof
(compassion   misplaced)
Inexorable   seer—
"Weep not for me
but for yourselves   and for your children"

Catastrophe?   indeed
not his
death   His death
lucidity   gift   judgment   triumph
Worse things await
the daughters of Jerusalem—
nightmares   daymares
horrors unspeakable
fall of Jerusalem
fall   of the daughters of Jerusalem

"And when he approached, he saw the city and wept
over it, saying, 'If you had known in this day, even you,
the things which make for peace! But now they have
been hidden from your eyes. For the days shall come
upon you when your enemies will throw up a bank
before you, and surround you, and hem you in on every
side, and will level you to the ground and your children
with you, and they will not leave in you one stone upon
another, because you did not recognize the time of your
visitation.' "

(Luke 19:41–44)

Over him   the women wept
on the Jerusalem road
for sight of him
Behold the man!
scorned   scourged to the bone
dragging in the filth
the crossed plank   symbol
of utmost degradation
He raises a hand
not in anger   reproof
gentle   calming
Better a misplaced grief
than none at all!
Let the tears fall   yes but
from right understanding

The Number 8 bus
He heaves aboard
on Jerusalem road
travel-worn   bone-weary
(how many miles   how many years!
meager belongings   bump   thump
down the swaying aisle
Does he seek a handout?
Does he offer a gift?

The coin withheld?
the gift refused?
For all the tears
(alas   his plight
that such things should be—)
Tears yes   but
for whom   whose sake?
whose loss   whose death?

Souls are faces
we
look alike   refuse alike
weep alike
die alike
Gratuitous   unsettling
"Weep not for me"
In fear and trembling
a question arises—
Shall the sons and daughters
of the daughters of Jerusalem
unto this generation—

shall we too
resemble our mothers
weep the wrong tears
rightful tears
for wrong reason?
tears abundant   a river of tears
for ancient wrongs
for Jesus long dead   long risen from death
No tears   no grief
upon present wrongs
no recognition
no wrath for the death
crossing our path
no *no* uttered
no gainsaying
death's dark empery
day upon Christian day

STATION NINE

The Final Fall

For I said, "May they not rejoice over me,
Who, when my foot slips, would magnify themselves
   against me."
For I am ready to fall,
And my sorrow is continually before me.

(Psalm 38:16–17)

"THIS IS   AN ACCIDENT REPORT
Under Police Barricade   Number 9
a man has fallen
he   or someone very like
reported injured   twice today
elsewhere   in the city"
(The staccato voice
crackling with tension   urgency)

"Identity unknown"
(identity too well known
homeless   John Doe)

Naming   being named
act   of biblical import—
at dawn of creation
a noble task   laid upon humans—
to "name all things"
Names infer   confer   vocation
Isaac   Daniel   Ezekiel   Jesus

"And out of the ground the Lord God formed every
beast of the field and every bird of the sky, and brought
them to the man to see what he would call them; and
whatever the man called a living creature, that was its
name. And the man gave names to all the cattle, and to
the birds of the sky, and to every beast of the field."

(Genesis 2:19–20)

The third fall
the stairs rise   straight up
tidal wave   nightmare
hydra-headed   pummeling
He lies there   hapless   helpless

This fallen one
We pause
we read   a larger meaning
indeed the name
Homeless J. D.
something   communal   tribal
"We have not here
a lasting dwelling"

And if perchance   supposing   otherwise
we wheel and deal   connive   compel
consuming   self-consumed—
solely intent on
"the things which are seen"—
we stand self-deceived

"Dwellers upon the earth"
dwellers   nowhere else
no hope   no soaring   no breakthrough
slaves drawing water   indentured
to the wheel of time

We pause
upon this fallen one
mortality   stasis
recumbent   bloody

Vital signs   all but extinguished
Yet
he will stand again
walk again
The end is not yet

We do not know the end
and we know
He does not know the end
and He knows
Mind spins about
somewhere   between
noble fiction
and sorry fact

Homeless J. D.
and homeless J. C.—
the Son of Man
"had not whereon
to lay His head"—
One day   His last
He fell to earth
and twice   and thrice
Nevertheless
went on   went on
to consequence
We hardly dare name it—
a borrowed grave—
all said   worst done—
Then
dawn burst
day broke
genesis
"He is risen"

A promise   nothing more
(hardly less)
cold comfort
under   a sorry flimsy marker
Police Barricade Number 9
A sorry   mime of death—
Meantime   all time
the promise   the counsel—

"I say to you, do not be anxious for your life, as to what you shall eat, or what you shall drink; nor for your body, as to what you shall put on. Look at the birds of the air, that they do not sow, neither do they reap nor gather into barns; and yet your heavenly Father feeds them. Are you not worth much more than they? And which of you by being anxious can add a single cubit to life's span? And why are you anxious about clothing? Observe how the lilies of the field grow; they do not toil nor do they spin, yet I say to you that even Solomon in all his glory did not clothe himself like one of these. But if God so arrays the grass of the field, which is alive today and tomorrow is thrown into the furnace, will he not much more do so for you, O you of little faith?"

(Matthew 6:25–30)

STATION TEN

The Stripping

Then you shall be brought low;
From the earth you shall speak.
And from the dust where you are prostrate,
Your words shall come.
Your voice shall also be like that of a
    spirit from the ground,
And your speech shall whisper from the dust.

(Isaiah 29:4)

Ten P.M.   Tenth Station
vast   warehouse of humans
the "City Shelter for Men"
airless   impersonal   a morgue
blazing with neon
like high noon in hell—
the hour of stripping   delousing   showering
"the rule upon admittance"

Winter night   many refuse
with frostbitten fingers   to lift
the door latch of hell—
(the alternatives
by no means   heavenly)—
brave the night cold
heat grates   doorways   subways

J. Doe   having endured
the Kafkaesque hours
scorn   contumely

eviction   judge   guards
having survived   barely
the pitiless   triple   tumble to earth
having walked the gauntlet
blank stares   black looks
more eloquent   than curses
having crawled through
the needle's eye—
such a feat   such ills
as would burn white
the beard of Job   in an hour—

Ten of the clock   strikes
Pared to his bones   bare flesh
J. D. pays afresh
the entrance fee of shame
in the house   of the near dead

"Possession   nine points of the law"
(Possessions   nine points of the law)
nonpossession   less than one point of the law
(that pitiful   condemned
fraction and fiction
"one point of the law")
derided   disappearing
in huffs and puffs
gavels and groans
of legal hounds
This tattered miscreant—
take him away!

Cots like morgue slabs
the realm of misery   multiplied

Two worlds   two cities
one
possessed   by possessions
(who owns what   what owns whom?)
get   greed   gloat
Then
this sad
recumbent   motionless   phalanx
the dispossessed   near dead

And over all
serene   afar
the moon   swells to a fullness
pascal moon   moon of deliverance
moonfire   spontaneously kindled
hillside to hill   across the world
signifying
Deliverance!

Not here   not yet
deliverance
not here   (the law impeding)
not yet   (the law impeding)
possession   impeding elsewhere
dispossession   impeding here

Pascal moon
moon of Gethsemane
bloodshot moon
moon of the blood of Christ
the tears of Christ
no merciful ray   alas falling
only "the Father's will"
like a hemlock brew
falling   filling to brim
"the cup   that will not pass"

Moon of the homeless
homeless moon   wandering moon
lantern of a seeking God
"Show me
in the tangled skein   cross-purpose
welter   chaos—
show me   one honorable mortal
I shall bless all"

Sleep   poor man
clean as a public corpse
multiplied   hundredfold
American hecatomb
Sleep   dream
granted at last
grudged   dole of sleep

The moon pauses
lingers
over that face
noble   violated
pauses
like a lantern held
like the held breath
of God the seeker
a wraith of hope
a dream passing over
deliverance   dawn

promises
godlike
eventual
after torment
delight
after scorn
vision
beatific

STATION ELEVEN

The Nailing

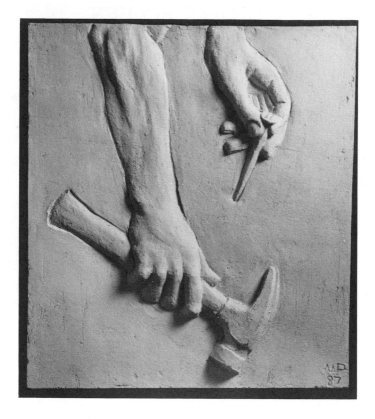

And when they came to the place called The Skull,
there they crucified him and the criminals, one on the
right and other on the left. But Jesus was saying,
"Father forgive them; for they do not know what they
are doing."

(Luke 23:33–34)

Eleventh Station
The nail marked "11"
Inventive minds   might conjure
eleven ways
to   "nail someone"
(and devil   take the hindmost)

The Stations   the final hours
of one   Hindmost
a mysterious Someone
hapless   homeless
pushed aside
bound   sentenced
delivered over

In light of this One
in light of ourselves
Station 11   nail eleven
(two hands poised
in mid act
of nailing someone)

might be thought
starkly
—pointed

Two hands   a hammer
a nail incised "11"—
closeup   concentrated glimpse—
the "national genius"
ready—

—a people
known   here and there   for
"nailing things down"
a people   creating
their own   for themselves alone
reductive   concentrated   easily grasped
(forever elusive)
universe
(good   evil   we   they   heaven   hell)
Two hands
building   producing   subduing   enhancing
owning   claiming   seizing—
grasp and clout   hammer and nail

You hear   in the night
the hammers   raised   lowered
a momentous heartbeat
household hammers   jackhammers   sledge
    hammers
the intractable world
nailed down!   everything in place!
    a place for everything!

Likewise
a different sound   though the same
the stacatto stutter   the shuddering earth
guns   bombs   cannons   missiles
testing!   testing!
warning!
a bellow   a sonic boom—
godlike   prevailing
"This place!   Our place!
Yield this place!   Leave this space!"—

A hoarse titanic roar
vibrating going   of the universe
airy splendor   demonic beauty
deserts split apart—
antitrinity
savior   death
"coming on the clouds"

(And the Hill of Skulls
grows of itself   an anti-
miracle   spawning
megadeath   mock Easter)

War   peace   hot war   cold peace—
everyone in place
a place for everyone!
high place   low place
everyone in place
especially
"if I had a hammer"—
the poor in place!

Name it   nail it
reality   nailed down
a majestic bird
pulled from its element
fastened   nailed
to a rotted wall—

How many ways
to crucify reality
to name and nail—
the homeless nailed out
nailed in
in   out   warehoused   evicted—
everyone in place!   a place for everyone!

Blessedly
"not clever for the next time
but wise forever"—
another word   another way

———————

"Because I delivered the poor who cried for help,
And the orphan who had no helper.
The blessing of the one ready to perish came upon me,
And I made the widow's heart sing for joy. . . .
I was eyes to the blind,
And feet to the lame.
I was a father to the needy,
And I broke the jaws of the wicked,
And snatched the prey from his teeth.

(Job 29:12-13, 15-17)

———————

STATION TWELVE

Death

It was now about the sixth hour, and darkness fell over the whole land until the ninth hour, the sun being obscured; and the veil of the temple was torn in two.

And Jesus, crying out with a loud voice, said, "Father, into thy hands I commend My spirit." And having said this, He breathed His last.

(Luke 23:44–46)

The terror of Gate 12
Station 12
Fear   trembling
overmastering

The gate
laid to a grid
time   no time
no exit
The word
dies in the throat—
death   dismemberment
(the scattering   not now
of paltry possessions
a different   more terrible
predicament)

No outcome
The impenetrable web
No earthly power   skill   summons
no congeries of these—
fabled medicaments   wonder drugs—
nothing avails
"He whom you love   has died"

Come   enter
the land named   Too Little
the hour named   Too Late

Speech gone   on the wind
hearing   sight
on the wind
now
dead   calm   the zone of zero

Death   great alas
susurration of grief
Sights   sounds   odors   voices
gone   perfume of memory!
faces loved   lost
Closed   closed   by invisible hands
the lid of the world   that sphere
whose heart is music   Now
stilling of music
"The rest is   silence"

"And the sound of harpists and musicians and fluteplayers and trumpeters will not be heard in you any longer; and no craftsman of any craft will be found in you any longer; and the sound of a mill will not be heard in you any longer; and the light of a lamp will not shine in you any longer; and the voice of the bridegroom and bride will not be heard in you any longer."

(Revelation 18:22–23)

FINIS
writ large
soul   body   mind   *finis*
The world   its wonders
ecstatic   an unfailing spring
whose glory
eyes   tongue   touch
sang—

Instruments we were   harmonies
strung to every wind
Alas   we are unstrung   gone
gone   (the gong persists   the bell of passing)
gone
as echoes go
or shadows come
when sun sets
All things   at sunset
merest shadow

Gate 12
In fear and trembling
enter there
Gate 12
the yawn   the beyond

Gate 12
Look long
look hard
(take courage!)
not to look
to look back
look away
is to lose all

A like warning and law
governs the art—
to make of death
executioner death
damned death
demonic death—
lighthearted interlude
"a little night music"—
to paint   a mortician face
on brute fact
—whorish
servitude of death

True art
deals otherwise

tosses our way
a golden sun
a beacon
a bezoar stone
a star

a hidden charge—
(run to it   run from it)—
explosive
truth

The Twelfth Gate
Vast unrelieved
horror of space
cruel simulacrum
of plenty and peace
mockery   misdirection
of the homing heart—

Stripped   dispossessed   disposed of
frail vessel of mortality
in seas of mischance—
tossed
like a curragh
in tides contrary
(the sorry hours
told   tolled)
the swamping wave
the thin edge—
J. D.
sleeps at length

Then
merciless   tender
imperious   final
a summons
and
"Into your hands
I commend my spirit"

The art
all trembling
traces—
"Come   beloved"—
head falls lax
heart   a drayhorse
flayed   uphill
halts in its tracks

Is this all of art
is this all of God?
the story entire?
No   only
"the things which are seen"

The art makes visible
"the things   unseen"
pondering   penetrating
"the things   which are seen"
By artful fiction
more strange than fact

by truth   by image
more real than real—
thus
things   dis-membered
(rags   bones   the rag and bone shop)
shall be   shall be
one to another
re-membered at last

therefore
alas
for
now—
alleluia
forever

STATION THIRTEEN

The Nameless One

See, O Lord, and look,
For I am despised.
Is it nothing to you all who pass this way?
Look, see if there is any sorrow like my sorrow. . . .
Because far from me is a comforter,
One who restores my soul;
My children are desolate. . . .
He has besieged and encompassed me with
   bitterness and hardship.
In dark places has made me dwell,
Like those who have long been dead.

(Lamentations 1:11–12, 16; 3:5–6)

Corner of Thirteenth and Nameless
The nameless one   goes under
who goes there   who lives there
who dies there?
Nameless

and above   and above
blank as God's brow
the hives
where humans dwell   do not dwell
no one to tell   not tell
Empty   boarded   shuttered   window
   after   window
wide-eyed   blank
dead eyes   stare past   the dead

"In my end   is my beginning"
Thus the story   nearly ended
ends
where it began
in the Land of the Blind
(the unafflicted   unaffected   affectionless
passersby   where it began
O you who pass by)

Not all pass by
"Let the little children
come to me   forbid them not"
A street   Thirteenth and Nameless
two waifs
unbidden   unforbidden

Grant the dead   a voice
the living had none
"I   inarticulate
spoken for   reported on
in death   as in life   or what passed for life
passive   as cobbles   underfoot
poked   prodded   ordered about
disallowed   ignored
a statistic   on a page
in a file   in a drawer
in an office   in a building
on a street   in a city
any page   any file   any anyway—
shunted about   catalogued   kept in place
a 'case'   an instance

faceless   voiceless
ground under   computerized
My passionate soul

"Now the computer
under 'J. D. Homeless'
goes blank   buzzes   'dead file'

"Nonetheless
the children   come to me
My soul lingers   recusant
no sorrow   like to my sorrow
I linger
in a blind window
a shell   a simulacrum
mockup of life
a curtain   waving   witlessly
like a flag of truce
in the hands of the dead
'I surrender   you win'

"Those children
my parched flesh
grateful   astonished—
tenderness   unwonted
a tear
springs in the desert"

Street children   children of ill luck
child John Doe   child Jane Doe
under the ominous
shadow and sign   Thirteenth and Nameless
a warning sign   a cross-arm
raised like a totem   portending
only disaster
"Run from here"
"Linger at risk"

They linger   risk
Where did he learn   who instructed her
In what hard school   Street of Ill Luck?
empty shells   blind windows
who the teacher   COMPASSION?

"I shall not
altogether die
until I praise
until I kiss my hand
until I place   my sorry nimbus
that predilected
vocation of misery
grown glorious
on those dear heads

"Children   for this favor
this coverlet laid
tenderly   on my
much abused bones—

I swear
by His death and mine
and your   and my
trek   through hell—
now worn   now weary
we shall make merry
in God's great realm"

All Things New

God shall wipe away every tear from their eyes; and there shall no longer be any death; there shall no longer be any mourning, or crying, or pain: the first things have passed away. And he who sits on the throne said, "Behold, I am making all things new."

(Revelation 21:4–5)

To the city morgue
officials   come running
distrait   dismayed
wild-eyed   stuttering
something going on here
who knows what
nothing of moment
rumors   wives' tales

Mors et vita   duello
death   life   in mortal combat

How say it   how declare
good news
after bad—
punishment annulled
penalty undone
Someone walks away
victorious
Someone walks toward—
companionable

"Behold
I come
soon."

(Revelation 22:7)

Finally
(no   from the beginning)
I see You
walk toward me
in your wounds
ragtag   nameless
J. D.   J. C.
those frail   speechless   bones
alight   as a phosphor
that face alight
those wounds

Your credentials—
dying   somberly
for others   they say
mors et vita   duello
then   they say
walking free

walking the cities   walking the ages
what a burden
pondus gloriae   weight of glory—

Tell the litany—
gratitude begrudged
fake and true vows
masses muttered
refusals   reprisals
guns   settling matters
crucifixes   images
graven   groveling
grislier than the event

Then
the "glory gap"—
larger than life   You
begetting less than life
And how measure up
to the measure laid
to the sorry human
mocking   surpassing—
how not dread
mors et vita   duello
conflixere   mirando
death   life   locked in mortal combat

O give us peace
dona nobis   pacem
any peace
any price

Only   in solitude
under heavy crisis

in passing insight
gone   soon as granted—
You come toward me
free   great God   free at last
accretions   fallen away
egos   husks
dead   by the wayside

Can one   befriend   a God?
the question   is inadmissible
Nevertheless
a fiery recognition
lights us—
broken by life
making our comeback

AFTERWORD

In November 1986 I began to create a series of reliefs in terra cotta to record scenes becoming more frequent every day on the streets of New York: a beggar on the bus, a man pushing a shopping cart with all his worldly belongings, a woman living in my subway station, passed and ignored by the milling, moving throngs of New York City.

I first took terra cotta—clay made from red earth—and pressed it into flat, eighteen-by-sixteen-inch rectangular forms. Then I built up and carved images out from the flat background. Half-scale drawings outlined each composition, but working the clay brought an intimacy and reality of its own. The wet clay responded to my touch in an almost human way.

Images of many other reliefs influenced my work—the cast of the Parthenon frieze at the University of Michigan Graduate Library, the Art Deco figures at the Rockefeller Center, the magical power of African carving, the everyday life in Egyptian friezes, the eternal stories in the reliefs of medieval churches. Then the immediacy of the streets took over, and my vision was sharpened by their barely controlled chaos—the dance of the crowd, hands reaching out, the urgent, whispering voices. Each message was different, but the struggle was the same. I began to realize I needed a central figure. What could I do?

The overall form of the series came from a childhood memory. I remembered learning about the last hours in

the life of Jesus, from his trial to the forced march through
the mocking crowds to his death. Why did no one help,
why did no one stop, no one cry out? At once, past and
present merged, and I recognized the reactions of that ancient crowd in myself—the hatred, the fear, and the shame
that make us turn away from the fallen. On the streets of
New York, I came face to face with a visitation.

Using the devotional form of the Stations of the Cross
caused me great trepidation. Raised in the United Church
of Christ, I left the church behind after high school. Its
answers never seemed to catch up with the rough and
tumble of life. But the images on the streets were so insis-
tent that I simply set out to record what I saw and hoped
for the best.

I was unprepared for the spiritual exercise that would
follow. In the early reliefs, large visual themes dominat-
ed—repeated patterns of buildings, stairs, grates, crowds
crushing the individual. But as the subject became more
familiar, the crowd began to recede and the central figure
came alive. Finally, as the mystery unfolded, I realized
that I was incorporating all I knew and loved into these
images: a revelation of my own mother's love for me (Station Four), the hands of my father, a carpenter (Station
Eleven), the awakening eyes of my four-year-old daughter (Station Thirteen).

The image of death—Station Twelve—was completed
early. The most difficult to conceive, it bore the strictest
responsibility to the savageness of living and dying on
the street. To follow the agony to the end, the figure had
to be completely shattered and all patterns had to be
broken to bring release.

Daniel Berrigan first saw photographs of the series when it was half-finished. His thoughtfulness and encouragement were of great help. Our collaboration brought the series through several more stages. When he said he didn't see many blacks, women, or children in the reliefs—the groups that make up the majority of the homeless—I was horrified. By aiming at the universal, I had unconsciously repeated the act of obliteration. Every unfinished piece was changed.

The image for Station One was still unclear. Dan suggested, "Why not the inside of a courtroom?" How appropriate for the homeless, so frequently crushed by the legal system, and also as a small marker of Dan's lifelong commitment to achieving social justice through civil disobedience. The image for Station Fourteen, the last relief, was left until the end. In my preliminary sketch, a draped figure lay on a stretcher, surrounded by people. Dan asked for something more, especially considering the extreme dismemberment of Station Twelve. At a loss for a more powerful statement, I finally recalled the ancient method of mixing figures in raised relief with those carved out in reverse. With the single rising figure carved into the background came a shock of recognition, and my part of the series was complete.

Margaret Parker